The Best Ships

Frank J. DiMaio
with Vicki Lindgren Rimasse

First Edition Design Publishing
Sarasota, Florida USA

The Best Ships
Copyright ©2021 Frank J. DiMaio

ISBN 978-1506-906-63-8 PBK
ISBN 978-1506-906-64-5 EBK

LCCN 2021921816

October 2021

Published and Distributed by
First Edition Design Publishing, Inc.
P.O. Box 17646, Sarasota, FL 34276-3217
www.firsteditiondesignpublishing.com

Front and Back Cover Photo Credits, Mike Maculley
Design by Nico DiMaio

To the memory of my late wife, Judith, and to Anastasia, without whom my journey to Bermuda would not have taken place.

Acknowledgments

There are many people to thank for their support, guidance, and love in connection with this book, and in my life.

First, a deep and heartfelt thanks to my father, Frank and my mother, Helen, who, by example, taught me valuable lessons about perseverance and hard work. Thanks also to my wonderful children, all of whom I am extremely proud, as well as my grandchildren. I hope my story inspires them.

To Mike Maculley, a second brother and fellow sailing and adrenaline junkie, thank you for knocking sense into me! I never would have completed the sail and fulfilled a promise without your friendship.

Thanks to Professor Anderson from Providence College whose lessons about poet James Joyce first sparked my interest in writing.

Thanks to Jennifer Worrell, educator, and writer, who wrote about my earlier attempts to complete my sail. Thank you for capturing the essence of my story through your vision and power of the pen. To the doctor in the Rhode Island emergency room who gave me a suture kit for my sail, a wonderful and much-needed gesture of support.

Thank you to my editor and collaborator, Vicki Lindgren Rimasse, who made the tone of my tale more hopeful and uplifting, and who put a blowtorch under my butt to help get this book completed. I look forward to our future collaborations.

Thanks to Mark Prestage, a great friend and fellow adventurer, who was brave enough to live outside the box and follow my "tie a rope around your waist and jump" instructions (detailed in Chapter 2: Seas-ing the day: Jumping off and Crash Landings). Thanks also to my brother Jim and cousin James for joining me on one of my first adult sailing voyages on my catamaran. You had no idea what was in store with me at the helm, but you hung in there!

Thanks to Jessie and Greg and the others who greeted me at the marina when I finally made it back from Bermuda. Thanks to Chris and his father whom I met during my respite in Paradise, who tried in earnest to get me to join them in their sail to the Azores; one day, gentlemen; it's still in my heart. Thanks also to my fellow travelers whom I met in Bermuda; our celebration was a once in a lifetime fete among ships that passed in the night.

Thank you to Yitzi Weiner and Pirie Jones Grossman who helped me share my story of healing after a dramatic life change through their publication, Authority Magazine, and to my publisher, Deborah Gordon Reagle of First Edition, who offered her expertise and guidance during the entire process.

Thanks to my Beta Readers, who helped make this book better through with their suggestions, including Helen, Jill, Matty, Art, my cousin James, Helene, and Judy.

Thank you to the bird and the Dolphins who joined me on the last legs of my journey, when all other communication broke down. Thanks also to my personal Senate; the parts of my personality that forced me to say "yes" even as others said "no," including the Adventurer, the Court jester, the Healer, the Educator, the Pragmatic, and Mr. Cranky Pants. You enrich my imagination and keep me crazy, and as the late Robin Williams said "You're only given a little spark of madness. You musn't lose it." Finally, thanks to Anastasia, gone but not forgotten. Without you, the sail to Bermuda would have been nothing more than an echo the wind left unreconciled.

Contents

Foreword

I met Frank (then known as "Fran") DiMaio (a/k/a Francesco James) in the 1970s, when he was in Chiropractic school and I was in law school; we both tutored through the study skills center at New York Institute of Technology, my Alma Mater. Frank was ridiculously handsome, and as a silly, giddy 22-year-old girl, he was swoon-worthy in my eyes, so much so that the first time we met I said, "I have no idea who you are, but I'm madly in love with you!" Unperturbed by the hyperbole, he calmly said "Thank you," and smiled. (It is unlikely that it was the first or only time a young lady expressed such sentiments; it was part and parcel of the curse of being handsome!) Despite my silly and over-the-top greeting, we hung out together from time to time. During one memorable encounter, he taught me a pain relief technique that helped me every month for years. You see, I suffered greatly from menstrual cramps, and the exercise he demonstrated helped to alleviate them. Over the years, I shared the technique with my crampy sisters. Midol be damned! It helped! Hallelujah! We lost touch until forty plus years later when reconnecting via social networking, sharing that we were both writers. While I was a published author, his manuscripts were in deep storage, and he deemed them not worthy of publication.

With consistent cajoling (of which my skills are renowned), I finally convinced Frank to share various manuscripts he had written. They were nothing short of brilliant: eloquent, rich with imagery, and captivating. One that stood out was the first version of this book. It was long, arduous, and heart wrenching and rife with grammar and punctuation *faux pas*. It was so powerful that I had a violent physical reaction after reading it, something I would not wish on anyone else. The segments about his sail to Bermuda, however, were entertaining and uplifting, so I had no choice but to continue cajoling until he agreed to publish them.

Having lost two close friends to breast cancer and no stranger to dark times myself, it became my mission to help Frank tell his story in a manner that would help others and shine a light at the end of the tunnel. The result is *The Best Ships*, a story of courage, perseverance, and the importance of friendship, summed up by an uplifting toast offered by Frank's friend and comrade in arms, Mike, from which the title of this book is lifted.

It bears mention that Frank is still ridiculously handsome, and as a silly 66-year-old girl, I remain enthralled by a "pretty face," although he insists that "men are not pretty! Men are handsome!" Sorry, Francesco; this is my note not yours!

All silliness aside, I have no doubt that *The Best Ships* will make you laugh, cry, and think, and remind you to call your best friends, if for no other reason than to share a laugh. As a side note, as of this writing, we are currently collaborating on several other books, including a children's book based on this one; stay tuned for updates.

Vicki Lindgren Rimasse,
Collaborator and Editor

Author's Note

If you have never sailed, you might not be familiar with terminology used in this story. A glossary is at the back of the book for ready reference.

Introduction

"The world is a great ocean, upon which we encounter more tempestuous storms than calms."

Edgar Allan Poe

My wife Judith died in 2004 after a courageous battle with breast cancer. Before she passed, I promised her that I would sail to Bermuda to raise money to support the cancer center where she was treated. Although I put up a brave front throughout her illness, playing the role of her Knight in Shining Armor, my armor was tarnished; I was a complete wreck. Thoughts of joining her were relentless. How could I go on? What would I do? It felt as though there was nothing to live for, dreams and plans that pulled me away from my incessant inner torment shattered into shards of regret. I was a man overboard, going down for the last time.

As I eventually came to realize, in addition to my fundraising efforts, the cure I was sailing for was more personal. I needed to embark on the journey to cure not only the sadness I felt upon losing a loved one, but also to banish the demons that had haunted me since childhood.

During the unspeakably dark period following her death, Judith spoke to me in a dream. "Listen," she said, "I am happy you came into my life. Live it! Live it to the fullest! Find peace in your heart that I am spiritually at peace, happy with no pain and can hear quite well. You are the shining spirit that touched my soul. Find a boat and live our dream."

And I did.

My "sail for a cure" came in many fits and starts, but I ultimately made it.

My hope for you, dear reader, is that my story will inspire you and bring you the same measure of courage that I derived from completing the trip. Life is short, joy is shorter; live it with a bone in your teeth, and never miss a chance to notice all the sails in the wind.

Chapter 1

Soon Enough, Scout

My fascination with the ocean began when Neptune gifted me with diamonds for the first time. I was a Boy Scout from childhood to young adulthood. It would make a nice homespun tale straight out of a Norman Rockwell painting to say that being a scout was my lifelong dream, but that would be a lie. As a

3

kid raised in the 1950s-60s, I followed the rules set for me by my parents and teachers. However, I was a desultory student; restless, a tad rambunctious, with a short attention span. As such, my parents thought scouting would be a healthy outlet for me.

I sometimes balked at the rules and regimentation but was "all in" the summer when sailing became an option at camp. First, learning to sail meant the chance to earn a merit badge, which would keep my parents happy. Secondly, stories of the sea had been a part of family dinners for as long as I could remember. My father and some of my uncles were Navy men. Moreover, growing up in New England, surrounded by water and boats made sailing a natural inclination, if not a birthright.

On the day of my first sail, I lay quietly in my tent when the abrupt sound of the bugler sang out reveille to the four corners of the camp, tearing through the early morning silence. A scene reminiscent of a *Three Stooges* skit would soon begin, as the seven scouts in my tent stirred, grunted, and made sundry audible noises and comments as a new day dawned. Scouts scurried about, fumbling with shoes and socks to be on time. As always, I was a bundle of nervous energy, even more so on that day than usual since I knew what lay ahead; my anticipation was palpable.

The troop met to discuss the day's itinerary following breakfast at the mess hall. Ours had the honor of being the first to swim that morning. The fog hung low across the lake, making it difficult to see the opposing shoreline. While the sun warmed the air, it punched holes in the mist, as blinding rays bounced off particles of fog unwilling to surrender to the sun's warmth. The early-morning breeze caused goose bumps, and shivering lips as we left the protection of the water.

As the troop hightailed back to the warmer climes of the camp, I shivered as much from the breeze as from anticipation. I would soon be venturing out on the lake in a boat much different from the canoe to which I was accustomed. The time had come for me to learn a new method of travel, harnessing the wind instead of my arms as a means of propulsion.

The instructor announced, "All those in the sailing class make your way to the docks! Do not forget! Put your life preservers on first!"

His instructions interrupted my steady gaze on the ripples across the lake courtesy of the early morning breeze, appearing like diamonds glistening in the sunlight. My heart pounded in my chest, palms sweaty, I moved quickly to the orders of the instructor's request making my way to the dock.

"O.K. scouts! We are going to start with some identification of equipment... "

I only half heard what he was saying.

"This tall pole is the mast, that one is the boom, and this is the tiller."

I continued to look back at the diamonds over my shoulder. The volume of the Instructor's voice escalated, interrupting my fixation on the shimmering ripples on the lake.

"Hey scout! Pay attention; you will be out there soon enough!"

However, once I saw the diamonds and felt the possibility of what the sea could bring, and the beauty and power of the wind, I was forevermore dazzled and transfixed.

Chapter 2

"Pull that thing. Pull that other thing. Sail Faster."

From the Princess Bride

Seas-ing the day: Jumping off and Crash Landings

My dreams of owning a boat were dry-docked until years later when I purchased a twenty-foot catamaran. She needed TLC, but overall, was a beauty. Built in England, she had mahogany decks and wooden cross members with wooden tillers. The mast stood twenty-six feet with a fully battened main sail and a forward jib. I happily toiled away until she was in perfect shape to take me on my first adult sailing adventure.

The day of my first voyage ticked all my boxes; fear, heavy breathing, sweaty palms, a pounding chest even my hands trembled.

The sudden jolt of hull speed came quickly, the windward hull rising from the water as the boat gained speed. Once the sails and hull were balanced it performed admirably, gaining speed in the building breeze to the point I passed a powerboat on plane. With no idea as to the speed of my vessel or the powerboats, I waved on my way by, smiling and giddy with joy. I had found my risk fix.

After a few solo excursions, I invited my brother and our cousin to sail around Jamestown Island in the middle of Narragansett Bay. The winds were light with moderate puffs of quick air just enough to bring a hull out of the water and get our adrenaline flowing. With three people on board, the cat hit speeds greater than when I sailed alone. We floated between islands and ventured into Newport harbor anchorage weaving between forty-foot vessels at anchor with the Martini crowd in the cockpit and their sexy two-piece offspring sunbathing on the forward deck. Some were topless, which required a second go around for another closer look. The captain or Commodore would wave us off and yell familiar slang. My response..." just admiring her lines Captain, admiring the hull's lines." All three of us laughed and dipped into the cooler for another cold one as we made our way out toward the open water around Beavertail Light at the southern tip of Conanicut Island. This is the mouth of the bay, where the ocean meets the two passages on either side of Jamestown Island. Depending on the time of day and current change, the waters can be challenging to maneuver for a small craft with no engine. I do not think either my brother or my cousin knew exactly what they had signed on for with me at the helm.

After a stretch of smooth sailing, the winds piped up and the seas got choppy. The cold breeze on my neck warned of things bigger than we were in terms of Mother Nature. The breeze signaled a squall, i.e., a strong wind and possible rainstorm lasting for a half an hour or so. To call the wind "strong" is somewhat of an understatement; it can gust up to thirty knots with shortened wave patterns to make life for a small vessel miserable. Well, misery we got! Unable to make the turnaround, we sailed further out into the storm. The gust and chop of the building sea wreaked havoc on the boat. The deck on one of the pontoons popped open and filled with water; then the rudder arm on the same side snapped under the pressure. We all had the fear of God on our faces. I slid down the canopy to gain control of the broken rudder. I lay on the hull, the opened deck between my legs gripping the edges with my feet for stability. I told the others to hold on and instructed them on how to control the mainsail. Our communication was short and to the point.

"Are we heading toward the beach?" I asked.

"Yes, there is someone waving at us," my cousin replied, "and he's saying something that I can't hear."

"Wave back!"

As the boat built up speed, my passengers sat high up on the pontoon out of the water. I was underwater with the pontoon using all my strength to stabilize the cat. My cousin was finally able to hear what the arm-waving man on the beach was saying.

"Damn!" my cousin said, "he says we can't come in here it is a private beach"

"We're coming whether he likes it or not." I screamed. "Hold onto the line. Not that one the other one, yes, when I tell you to release it, we will beach this rocket and be safe." The moment came quickly, and my cousin reacted perfectly as we sailed up onto the beach eighteen feet from the water line.

The now irate person repeated his comment about owning the beach and I laughed at him.

"If we were able to put her somewhere else fine, but this was our only option, given the squall and the damage we sustained," I said, pointing to the broken rudder and the open deck seam. Clearly disgruntled, he said nothing, storming off.

My cousin fell to his knees and kissed the beach, happy to be on dry land. I told him to pull the drain plug for the pontoon by lifting the access panel. Upon doing so, he said, "There are blue fish in here. We must have traveled through a school of them in our path toward the beach!"

"Are any big enough to eat?"

"No. Most are the size of sardines."

I lay on my back looking up at the blue sky left behind by the storm and laughed hysterically.

It was by then too late to retrieve the boat, so we left it for another day. My cousin and brother were both happy to be alive. I smiled with the satisfaction of another adventure under my belt...like any adrenaline junkie...I wanted more and more. Therefore, I later went on to larger sailboats and continued my junkie ways out on the coastlines of New England for my fix.

No one in their right mind would have sailed with me again, nor would I have sailed again myself. However, time heals all wounds, and when the weather is right, sailing on the coastal waters of New England is exhilarating. All one needs to do is point the front of the boat and say, "Let's go out there." Set the sails, lock the wheel, move forward, and sit on the bowsprit. So, I spent as much time as possible on the water, my back to the forward sail, legs dangling over the bow sprayed by the splash of seawater as the boat sailed itself, to somewhere out there away from land.

At times bored by the sleepy motion of the boat, the adrenaline fix I wanted was elusive. Of course, every intelligent individual has a conversation with himself or herself now and again, don't they? This was a perfect time. Hell, no one would hear. Therefore, I called upon my Senate, the various sides of myself, all of whom have distinctive personalities. *Inter alia*, there is the Pragmatic, the Contrarian, the Court Jester, and the Instigator. Banter filled the void; I was a Borscht Belt comedian sharing my schtick with the other versions of myself, those meshuggeners. The boat was my stage, and my audience the ocean.

Tying up a line at the mast, balancing with legs well spread apart for stability, I sat on the cabin roof for comfort facing the forward sail, full open along the side of the boat. The bottom edge was a foot above the roll of the ocean waves as they coursed along the hull. Wondering how the boat would act if I sat in the sail, I stood up and leaned against the lifeline. Returning to the cockpit, I changed the sail and steering position to accommodate the weight shift and lock the wheel. It was pure folly to think I could do this. With the devil on one shoulder and the angel on the other saying "Do it...Don't do it..." back and forth, ultimately the devil won; I threw caution to the wind, wrapping the line I had been rolling up around my waist, yelled, "Geronimo" and jumped into the sail.

Chest-deep in water, I sat in the sail as the boat continued its course, heeling so much the edge of the deck was submerged. Although it crossed my mind that the boat could turn hard and throw me over the deck, miraculously, it did not happen. She continued and I sat back into the sail getting drenched and loving every minute of it. Another adrenaline fix was in the books. Yippee!

I realize that this might sound childish. But the excitement of doing something totally outside the box energized and exhilarated me.

Soon I had the opportunity to share my new favorite fun activity with friends. They joined me for a sail and childish was the cry of freedom. Being towed behind the boat on a torpedo typically used behind a powerboat supplied the perfect laugh out loud moments of hijinks. One passenger, Mark, spoke freely about the enjoyment everyone was experiencing and expressed an enthusiastic and heartfelt thank you.

I said, "It's not over yet." The wind was perfect; I directed him to untie the line from the mast and presented my case for total relinquishment to live outside the box. He agreed, such a trusting fellow.

"OK, Mark, wrap the line around your waist."

He complied.

"Now this is the crucial part. See that sail in front of you?"

"Yeah," he replied.

"Jump into the pocket of the sail with your back to it."

"You're out of your mind!" he laughed.

"Yes! As a matter of fact, I am. That's the very point of living outside the box. So, just jump!"

He did, yelling and screaming, adrenaline coursing through him, getting everyone riled up. To this day, it is a go-to story that he recounts at gatherings of family and friends. A good day of sailing was had by all.

Chapter 3

"I drank to drown my sorrows, but the damned things learned to swim."

Frida Kahlo

Man Overboard

In the months following my wife's death, I descended into the abyss, drowning in grief; I was a basket case. Since I had quit my job to care for her during the final stages of her illness, I was unemployed, with no plans, and no direction.

After an extended period of solitude and assorted miseries, I sought solace with my family. A boisterous group, I hoped that spending time at a dinner table with food, family and friends would supply a reprieve from the escalating hopelessness that clouded my existence.

With that in mind, I joined a group of family and friends at a local steak restaurant. The evening started out fine until the familiar dragon reared its ugly head and extinguished my solace. As the others read their menus and engaged in small talk, an anxiety attack consumed me. I began to shake and had to hold on to the sides of the table to steady myself. Soon I was sweating uncontrollably. My white shirt, newly pressed for the occasion, was drenched within seconds.

After what seemed like an eternity, the women at the table noticed that I was in distress.

"Are you ok?" my mother asked. "You're sweating!"

"It's male menopause, ma."

Satisfied with the explanation, or perhaps to divert the attention away from my obvious distress, dinner resumed. I ordered a steak, choked it down, made it through the evening, and then descended back into my period of isolation.

Over time, through prayer, faith, and sheer determination, I pulled myself out of the darkness and began, in earnest to plan my sail, remembering the impetus for the journey. After years of treatment and other health issues complicating her recovery, Judith had come to peace with the idea that she would die. She was ready; I was not. With a view towards providing something positive to others and their families in similar situations, we first considered planning a day of sailing for cancer patients and their spouses. Judith's paralegal training put a kibosh on that plan, however, due to potential liability issues. The final plan of action, and her final wish, was for me to take a solo sail to Bermuda. It would be a fitting memorial to our mutual love of sailing, and the courage shown by her, and all cancer patients and their families.

Soon after, while visiting my home state of Rhode Island for Thanksgiving, I found the perfect craft - a Baba 35, named *Anastasia*. As fate would have it, the boat was for sale at a much lower price than it should have been. The owner's wife was selling it because of her husband's death. The parallelism was uncanny.

However, a month later, I had a moment of doubt, two days before the deadline to say yes or no to the deal. I had limited funding, and with my escalating fears I called the broker and left a message I would be backing out of the deal.

I felt a sense of relief after hanging up the phone, followed by a sudden jolt. Yelling out to myself in the car during a drive, one of the members of my inner Senate spoke to me. "What are you doing Frank? This was your wife's dying wish."

I backed out of backing out of the deal and was soon *Anastasia's* new owner.

Despite my new resolve, I dragged my feet a bit. Six months passed, and I did not feel anything in the way of order in my life. For a brief time, I traveled up to Virginia to spend time with a woman I met at church. Although we hit it off, her fear about my unsettled spirit and my fixation on making the journey to Bermuda ended the relationship before it ever really began.

"I don't understand why you have this need to do this," she said.

"It is what Judith and I loved to do together. I made a promise and I intend to keep it."

"A promise," she repeated, still not understanding. "You could die out on that damn ocean; can't you see that?"

"Yes, I can, and it's a risk, because I love life! I love life so much I don't want to leave it any sooner than I am scheduled to. But Judith told me she would help me, and I believe that."

The responsibility of choice came into the equation. Should I cast aside a promise or change my direction because of feelings stirred inside out of the desire to be with someone? I eventually retreated out of fear, and the relationship ended before it began.

Forging ahead, I began to prepare *Anastasia* for our journey.

Chapter 4

"Watch the little things; a small leak will sink a great ship"

Benjamin Franklin

Inauspicious Beginnings

The sail to Bermuda came in fits and starts, with various and sundry setbacks large and small, including mechanical issues, storms, and electronic meltdowns. For the sake of brevity, I will share details of only the most significant.

The Faulty Fan Belt Incident

On the morning of my first attempt to complete my mission, I left the Bay of my youth where many adventures had taken place along the shorelines and coves. It had been fifteen years since I last sailed these waters; in good weather and bad, rain or shine, it did not matter.

With the sail in place, I went to the bow and untangled the lead line for the roller furling, as *Anastasia* moved ahead with the wind. I turned to look back toward the cockpit and saw smoke billowing out of the companionway. I rushed back, quickly shutting down the engine and began to open all the hatches with a fire extinguisher in hand expecting the worst. There were no flames and what appeared as smoke was steam. I checked the hose connectors; the alternator belt had broken causing the engine to overheat, spewing coolant from the vent hose all over lines and equipment in the storage compartment.

Grabbing another belt and my tools from the parts locker, I put the new belt under tension and the alternator slid off the guide bar. After digging around, the problem became clear; the new belt was the wrong size. After a temporary fix, my only choice was to return to the dock for repairs, so I motored back, arriving six hours after my original departure. Once the repair was completed, I spent a few days motoring around the bay to ensure that everything was working properly, and set another departure according to the five-and seven-day forecasts. The weekend weather was favorable into the following week with thunderstorms and damaging winds up to sixty miles an hour inland and along the Connecticut coast.

I left in the early hours of the morning, alone on the dock but for two ducks sending me off.

"I want to thank Mr. And Mrs. Duck for coming out so early in the morning to see me off this second time. In recognition of your support, I would like to present you with these small morsels of bread to start your day on a full belly. Thank you."

That said, I followed the same procedure as I had the last time and headed for Virginia. The weather was glorious, with building breezes pushing the boat along at a good clip. I headed south to give *Anastasia* plenty of room from the impending storms over the coast. I expected a straight shot, with no stops, just the commercial traffic forty miles off the coast and me. The breeze topped out at 23 knots with *Anastasia* living up to her heritage, taking the seas in a kindly manner. With only one reef in the main and the foredeck sail, we covered about eighty-seven miles over ground by sunset.

The Kidney Stone Stall

Suddenly, I had the urgent need to take a leak, and upon doing so, I saw that my pee was red. Since I had no pain on urination and no back pain, the symptoms signaled either a kidney stone or an infection. I had to make a game time decision to turn back or forge ahead, with three days of travel left. A kidney stone would not pose a problem, but an infection would be another matter. Three days without treatment could turn an infection into a major health issue. I decided to play it safe and travel back to Rhode Island, which was only 14-16 hours away.

Reefing the main again in preparation for an evening run I turned the radar on, setting the 24-mile alarm to wake me in the event another vessel broke across the radar line. I took a nap with an egg timer next to my ear.

Arriving back in Rhode Island, the owner of the marina was nearby. When he saw me, he shook his head from side to side.

"Another problem Frank?"

"I'm pissing blood, I think I have a kidney stone."

"Geez, what next? When did that start?"

"Last night around 9:00. Where is the nearest Emergency room?"

"Down on the Avenue. Maybe someone is trying to tell you something!" He declared with the interest and guiding intent of a parent.

"Thanks." I said nothing in response to his second comment as I pulled off my foul weather gear, threw it down in the cockpit and headed for the truck.

When I arrived at the emergency room, after waiting for what seemed like hours, the doctor on call entered the room.

He asked when the pain started.

"Last night, when I was sailing to Virginia," I said. "I suspect it's a kidney stone, and if I had medication to take, I would have taken it, but in case it was an infection, I thought it best not to take any chances."

"How do you know all this medical stuff?."

"I am a Chiropractic physician."

His eyes widened and he nodded in acknowledgement of my training. After reviewing my symptoms and reinforcing my diagnosis, he concluded that the pain was indeed caused by a pesky kidney stone.

I then gave him the Readers' Digest explanation of my plan to sail to Bermuda to raise money for breast cancer awareness.

"Do you have a crew?"

"Nope; sailing solo."

"That's risky! Do you have everything you need?"

"I've been putting together a medical kit for my journey. I have more equipment than most EMTs. The only thing missing is a suture staple kit."

He listened attentively, nodding his head.

"Well, sail or no sail, good cause or not; you need to stay put for a week and let your body pass those stones."

"That is not what I wanted to hear Doc," I laughed.

"Right now, you have no other choice."

With that, he put his hand on my shoulder, told me to sit back and relax, and left the room.

I was still in immense pain, so relaxing was not an option. I felt that I had been a tad disingenuous, in not revealing that my days as a chiropractor had ended abruptly after a freak accident. When lifting weights with a friend, I sneezed at the same time I was putting a weight back on the rack, falling to the floor. Because of my hands-on method of treating patients, I was unable to perform the techniques I had learned in Chiropractic school, and as such, my thriving practice dissolved within 18 months. But that was another story for another day, and I feared that if he heard about that ordeal, he might try to discourage me from the trip I knew I had to take, one way or another.

When the doctor returned to the room, he handed me a prescription and a staple suture kit.

I was floored. His simple act of kindness was both moving and encouraging, so I stayed put long enough for the stones – and the latest delay – to pass.

Third Time was *Not* the Charm

My window of opportunity to leave for Bermuda was beginning to close. The National Hurricane Center predicted an active season, and I should have been in Virginia three weeks prior. I passed the kidney stone without discomfort, waited one more day as a precaution, and planned my departure time according to the tide.

The night before I left, I spent the evening with my parents and some of their friends. The questions started to fly my way about the trip, the weather, and the earlier incidents that caused my repeated returns. My mother began her cross-examination calmly at first, but her intonation grew steadily louder and more vehement as the conversation progressed.

"Frankie! Why can't you take someone with you on this trip?"

"Because I want to challenge myself." I responded softly but firmly.

"Don't you think that is foolish?" she asked, more as a statement than a question.

"No," I replied.

She shook her head, her lips pressed together, her eyes showing signs of concern. However, she nodded in silent acceptance. Having raised me, she knew that resistance was futile; I am, always have been, and always will be hardheaded; a *capatosta* according to Italian slang. When someone says, "hell no" my knee-jerk reaction is to say, "hell yes!" Remember the cartoon about a Coyote chasing a Roadrunner? One running gag involves the Coyote falling from a high cliff. After he goes over the edge, the rest of the scene, shot from a bird's-eye view, shows him falling into a canyon so deep that his figure is eventually lost to sight. This is followed, a second or two later, by the rising of a dust cloud from the canyon floor as the Coyote hits. And in the next scene, he rises again, to continue chasing his nemesis. That's pretty much me in a nutshell.

My dad piped up with a comment of experience, having been in the Navy during WWII on the Destroyer, the USS Bache (DD-470).

"Son, you are crazy going out there alone! You have no idea what the Atlantic can stir up. It tossed a Destroyer around like a cork when the weather got bad."

I remembered the stories he told me as a child about the North Atlantic and battles from the War. I got goose bumps thinking about 40-foot waves and my little cork on the water.

The next morning as I was preparing to leave, I began my usual dialogue with myself.

"OK, two attempts down, the third time is the charm Frank, right?"

I continued the conversation as I filled my water tanks and topped off the fuel in preparation for my departure. This time I left at 3:00 P.M. rather than in the morning. It was getting dark as *Anastasia* passed Block Island, heading for the open ocean. The winds were light, giving me a chance to get a couple hours of sleep with the radar set again on the usual 24-mile alarm. The evening went by without incident.

"Not bad headway Frank considering the light breeze overnight!"

After a while, the battery gauge showing the strain from the evening electrical needs was my signal to start the engine to charge them up. A half hour later, the engine alarm went off. After checking the belt, gauges, and electrical connections, the alternator turned out to be the culprit.

"Here we go again, what else can go wrong?"

Shutting down the engine, I cleaned the connectors on both the batteries and the alternator and started it up again. The gauge showed a slight improvement but was on the edge of the yellow range. There was no other choice, but to shut it down and sail to the nearest port, which turned out to be Barnegat Light, New Jersey.

My voyage plan and time of arrival put me at the lighthouse at 2:00 in the morning - not the best time to be making landfall in an area of shoals, particularly with no local knowledge of the area. Hence, I sailed for 6 hours then put the anchor light on for the rest of the night with the foredeck sail back winded and the rudder over.

The next morning my, GPS and chart work showed I was 23-miles off the coast. After tying up at the marina, the office gave me information about the nearest repair shop. Once the repair was completed, I set sail on the morning tide. Leaving the channel and the lighthouse in the distance, I headed east. The weather was about to change, and my goal was to be as far from land as possible when the gale force winds hit the coastline. In theory, I would be outside of the wind line since the system was following a northeasterly direction. Of course, that didn't happen. The storm hit anyway causing me to stay at the helm through the night with a blacked-out moonless sky, sailing by feel and watching the bow lights disappear into the wave trough up to the foredeck. I had set up my gale rider for deployment during the day, after getting the weather report about a gale advisory off the Delmarva Peninsula out to 20-nautical miles; it was time to put it to beneficial use. I fed out the rider with two hundred feet of line off my stern, hoping to match the wave step. I was, however, unable to see the waves in the continuous heavy rainfall that followed behind the gale force winds gusting up to thirty-eight knots.

I would not know whether the two hundred feet of line was right or not until I could check it in daylight. The storm continued throughout the following day well into the evening. The rider was OK, not best, but that was all the line I had to spare. The seas were confused, with froth spewing off the wave crests from the wind's force.

Some thirty hours later, I was nearing the entrance to Chesapeake Bay 38 nautical miles away to the southwest. I don't remember dozing off, but a sudden bang on the hull, and the boat pitching violently to the starboard bolted me upright in the cockpit. It was 2:30 a.m. The ship had run aground, beating the hull as it laid on its side bouncing across an apparent sandbar. The boat abruptly righted itself, my depth gauge reading thirty-three feet, so I wondered what I just hit. I ran forward dropped the anchor, setting it quickly. I returned to the cockpit and the depth gauge still read thirty-three feet. I checked my position on my GPS and charted it.

I could not believe my eyes. I had made landfall near the tip of the Eastern shore, and I could see the Cape Charles light off in the distance to the west. The chart showed I was anchored in an inlet, and any land or tree shadows were not visible on the shore. The bar surrounded the mouth of the inlet on the chart with the depth reading five feet down to two feet then back up six feet.

The next morning, I climbed into the cockpit and saw that the shoreline was only fifty feet off my stern, surrounding the boat like a horseshoe. I was amazed at the surrounding mass of low scraggily trees and scrub brush; it explained why the Lighthouse at Cape Charles was so visible and the shoreline impossible to see. I jumped into the water to check the depth, standing on tiptoes beside the boat with the water up under my nostrils. The tide chart on board showed the area would be in a flood tide soon. I began to brainstorm a way out of the situation.

"All right Frank, you have two anchors but no dinghy. What can you do to work your way closer to the sand bar before attempting to power out of the inlet?" my inner voices asked in unison.

I worked with the tide by swimming an anchor lashed to a life vest out toward the sand bar setting it with the winch. The best plan would be to pull in the first anchor, swim the second anchor past the first anchor then drop it, set it, and retrieve the first anchor. I estimated it would take me three swims to get the boat close enough to the bar to see the outer edges and evaluate what I saw with the chart, and the depth of the water I would be standing in. It meant more work than running the engine to maneuver around and potentially being stuck on an uncharted bar in the inlet caused by shifting currents and storms depositing sand.

The chart showed a narrow possibility of escape across the southern aspect of the sand bar. I walked the length of it until the depth fell off to my chest and neck. The chart was correct; there was a narrow escape route. I waited for high tide to make my getaway, steering *Anastasia* in a zigzag pattern to take advantage of the cresting wave structure to carry me above the sand bar, only to come crashing into it as another wave went by. The shudder through the hull when the keel struck was unnerving, but I was making progress.

As I cleared the last wave, the water became calm, and *Anastasia* settled into a smooth motion along the water. I pulled the remaining anchor rode aboard and secured it. I had finally escaped the danger of the beating, aground on the beach. The severity of such an incident could easily rip a keel off a sailboat or smash a hull into pieces from pounding against the hard sand and rocks of the beach.

I plopped myself down with a sigh of relief. Not bothering to raise the sails, I motored my way into Chesapeake Bay, pulling into Little Creek near Norfolk. After settling in, the boat was hauled out to assess the damage on the keel and hull below the waterline. Amazingly, the damage was minimal; some bottom paint had scraped off, and that was the extent of it. *Anastasia* and I spent the next month on blocks out of the water. I replaced my gauges with a new system, as I certainly could not trust the old one.

By the second week of July, the hurricane season had heated up. Tropical storms were hitting Florida, and my window of opportunity for the sail slammed shut.

I was crestfallen, a sense of failure overwhelming me. I regressed into my cave deeper to isolate and insulate myself.

Chapter 5

"Life is a shipwreck, but we must not forget to sing in lifeboats"

Voltaire

Red Flags to White Flags

Even at my best, I am not outwardly approach-able. Scratch that. I can be downright cantankerous, argumentative, and impossible to read. Like screen legend Greta Garbo, I often "vant to be alone" with my demons and dragons. After three failed attempts to sail, I lived on my boat in Virginia and spent my free time drinking at Sara's Pub. Once I sat at the bar, Sara or her husband Frank would wordlessly put a Guinness Stout in front of me. I would then sit in silence all evening, but for occasional small talk with random strangers about the weather or sports.

Despite my desire for solitude and anonymity, I became somewhat of an institution at Sara's, and the regulars learned a bit about my life, one of whom was Mike Maculley. Boisterous, full of piss and vinegar, and blessed with the gift of gab, Mike could always be counted on to belly up to the bar and regale people with a joke or a tall tale or two. One evening as I was finishing off my second beer and getting ready to leave, he approached me.

"I hear you have a boat at Southhall Marina, and you like to sail," he said, with enthusiasm and brio.

"Yes," I said with finality in my voice that discouraged any further discourse.

"OK, then," Mike said, reading my well-telegraphed "go away" subtext. He went to a table to rejoin his friends.

Even ogres such as I feel bad for offending others, as the grumpiness is more about me than about them. Hence, I picked up my drink and joined Mike and his group at the table. Bit by bit I emerged from my self-imposed iron bars and rejoined the living, in fits and starts.

By and by, Mike and I grew as close as brothers, and eventually, the grueling preparations for my sail to Bermuda were underway. Mindful of Murphy's Law, i.e., whatever can go wrong will go wrong, we set about to tune the rigging, replace worn lines, and perform general checks on engine systems, batteries, et al. Everything went according to plan, and I was ready to set sail again.

In early June, preparations for my departure were on a final checklist. Mike gave the rigging a final adjustment. A check on the weather showed no indications that any major difficulties would be met during my first day of sailing.

Mike took his sailboat along, taking pictures, as I made my way towards the mouth of the Chesapeake Bay. The winds variable at 15-25 knots, were perfect for *Anastasia* with her weight around 25,000 pounds after adding the supplies and extra tools.

I left with a jubilant heart, finally on my way, with the blessings of God in my purpose and the blessings of friends for a good and safe journey under sail. I made my first waypoint in the Territorial Sea and Contiguous Zone in the early evening hours east of the Chesapeake Horn and light.

The sky ahead was clear with a steady breeze and moderate seas when a mariner warning came over the radio from the Coast Guard that a storm was approaching with 7–9-foot seas and severe winds moving southeast from the Eastern shore of Virginia, "saying seek immediate shelter, don't leave port." Looking back over my shoulder a solid line of blackness consumed the western sky with a distinct line of demarcation. The night began to match the darkness of the storm, showing the stars and the moonlight. Heat lightning flashed through the blackness, visible every couple of seconds.

I turned *Anastasia* into the wind and began to prepare for the oncoming weather. It was suddenly upon me at the same instant, my attempts to roll up my forward sail futile. The upper third was twisted and left itself exposed to the wind. Moving quickly forward, I tethered both my safety-lines, one to the jack line, the other to the lifeline and began to lower my foredeck sail and mainsail. The third of the upper forward sail still taking on wind began to turn the boat, leaving the main vulnerable to jibe. Quickly dropping the foredeck, I began to release the main and the boat was propelled into an unexpected power jibe from the wind shift. This took the mainsail from its position over the gallows towards the Port side. In that split second, the mainsheet traveler failed to hold the boom and it sailed into the rigging on the port side, breaking the spreader from the force of the wind against it. Standing at the mast on the starboard side with the main halyard in my hand, I watched in terror as the boom forcefully hit the rigging in front of me.

At that point, the boom swung dangerously free with the mainsail still taking the full force of the increased wind. There was no time to stay forward and hope to lower the main. Returning to the cockpit, I retrieved some line to secure the boom at the vang and winch it back to a point over the gallows while powering into the wind. With the headsail still taking wind, a controlled maneuver was difficult. The lashing of the vang was not enough to bring the boom under control, as it swung violently from side to side with me ducking and bobbing, simultaneously preparing control lines for lashing the boom down.

The mainsail began to pop sail slides as it continued to take a beating from the wind. Then it happened, it ripped, and the rest of the slides let go and the main halyard snapped clean following the sail, going over the port side. The boom still flailed in the wind, as I pulled what was left of the main on board. The lines were in place to secure the boom and I tried to gain control. This little challenge lasted about an hour as the storm continued to rage around *Anastasia* with seas from 7–9-foot rollers changing to 7–9-foot chop breaking over the decks.

Once everything was lashed, tied or I was sitting on it, I headed back to port. It was critical to keep the wind on the starboard side for as long as possible since there was no upper lateral support for the left side of the mast above the spreaders. I clipped two free halyards to a deck cleat one was for my foredeck sail the other for the spinnaker halyard. This was the only available means of upper support I could give the mast. My only hope was it would sustain the lateral movement. The fury of cresting waves left a dramatic trough, and the stern fell leaving me hanging in the air for a split second above the wheel and pedestal returning with a new crest beneath it and slamming me into the wheel as if straddling a horse, at the same time avoiding the aggressive banter of the boom. The seat, I would have preferred *been wider*. I knew how a gymnast must feel when making a bad landing on the parallel bars or the balance beam. I continued to feel the results of the impact for the better part of two weeks. The effects of this quickly building low pressure lasted through the evening without any signs of diminishing. The cresting waves continued to break over the decks in steep chop with the bow burying itself up to the foredeck. The only lights visible up front was from the phosphorescence. The steep pitching of *Anastasia* continued through the night as I approached the mouth of the Bay and the transitional zone.

So occupied by keeping an eye on the mast and spreader, I did not notice smoke building in the cabin. The first hint was in my nostril of hot fluid or oil odor. I looked at the tachometer; it was buried at 3000 RPMs with *Anastasia* making 3.5 knots in gusts 45 to 50 knots. Locking the wheel, I went below to check the belts. Everything was in order but there was smoke coming out the opening. I returned to the helm and cut the engine to 2000 RPM's and turned one or two points off to port to reduce the severe pitching and ride the waves more effectively.

Sometime the next morning I was close enough and in the protection of the inner side of the Bay bridge tunnel to get signal on my cell phone to call Jessie and Greg, two fellow sailors on *So Wen Sa* and *Yoohoo*. When Jessie answered the phone, he was a bit confused since we were supposed to have a rendezvous over the Single Side Band radio at nine o'clock the previous evening. Since I had not answered, they assumed I was busy. They did not know how busy until they helped me back into the slip upon my return a few minutes before dawn.

After a futile attempt to sleep for a few hours, I set about to assess the damage, and clean things up around the boat. The confusion of lines and mainsail left me wondering how I had been able to maneuver about without tripping myself in the darkness. The damage was extensive. It included a broken spreader mount, a failed mainsheet traveler, a shattered halyard, a ripped main with broken sail slides the full length of the sail except those below my reef points and tears from splintered rod battens. Oh, and the headsail UV cover needed stitching attention as well as a tear in the leach of the foredeck sail.

Reflecting on all the red flags, I was ready to raise the white one and surrender...

Mike Maculley Photo Credit Francesco James

Chapter 6

"It is time to get drunk! So as not to be the martyred slaves of Time, get drunk; get drunk without stopping! On wine, on poetry, or on virtue as you wish."

Charles Baudelaire

A Dry Sail

A year later, I was back to Square 1, the wind now completely out of my sails. I found work on a tugboat, and spent most nights at Sara's, drowning my sorrows and eating like a condemned man, putting on weight, and putting my Bermuda sail aspirations into deep storage.

One night, as I was on my third of many Black and Tans, Mike confronted me.

Without preamble, he said, "Frank where is the fire that spilled out of you a year ago?"

"I think it was *beaten* out of me," I said with flat affect.

He hauled off and punched me in the arm, hard.

"I can't accept that as a reason!" he yelled. "What do I have to do - beat you into remembering your promise? Look at you – toiling away on a tugboat and coming back looking like a beached whale, thirty pounds heavier and your tail between your legs."

That was all it took; my wake-up call. My veins grew fat with blood as I regained the fire and desire of my journey, remembering the reason for the sail. Although I was hoping for an uneventful and casual sail to Bermuda, I wanted to be challenged as an homage to my late wife's courage and strength during her ordeal. I began preparations to try again, more determined than ever before.

Mike and I continued our brotherly banter. As I rubbed my arm post-punch, Mike continued his tirade, loud and clear. The trip was no longer a "maybe someday" – it was a "now." We strategized on the best time to leave, and what needed attention on the boat pre-sail. When we get together, the Black and Tans take a back seat to our friendly boisterous natures. So as not to be topped by Mike, I had a plan, a devious one at that. As vociferous as Mike can be, I can be calculating. I decided to tell him it was going to be a dry sail; no drinking allowed. I took a long pull on my beer and started in.

"Ok, brother here is the deal about Bermuda. You have a choice of direction. You can travel from Virginia to Bermuda or from Bermuda to Virginia, but not both. The sail is my personal challenge and though your wiry Scottish butt and ability to scurry up the mast when needed is a godsend, you can only go *one way*. So, your choice brother."

He chose to go from Virginia to Bermuda.

"Excellent," I said. "Now there is one other matter requiring discussion."

"What is that?" Amid his sip I let him have it.

"It will be a dry sail. No alcohol. Completely dry," I said, completely dryly.

He spit his beer out like hot sauce all over the bar. Those around the bar let him have it for not holding his drink, and laughter was contagious at Mike's expense.

"A dry sail?" he repeated, wiping off his face and the bar with cocktail napkins. "Kill me now!"

"That is the deal. If you don't take it - kiss this adrenaline junkie opportunity goodbye," I warned.

"Nothing?" "Nothing?!," he repeated.

"Take it or leave it, brother," I said, sipping my beer for emphasis.

"You do realize that I'm Irish and Scottish and libation is in my blood. I will respect your wishes, but it might not be pretty."

"Agreed," I concurred, motioning for the bartender to bring Mike a drink to replace the one he had spewed out. "Better drink up now while you still can."

The final preparations for the trip to Bermuda passed in slow motion as the time to leave got closer. During our final check Mike found a glitch in the steering system, which left us to sail without the benefits it would have provided. The situation was not dramatic in terms of necessity, as the alternative was for the two of us to take shifts at the helm. The repair would be on the agenda when we arrived in Bermuda.

We left Hampton, Virginia on Memorial Day weekend. The evening waters within the Bay were calm with little wind to drive *Anastasia* along. I had the first six-hour shift and motored my way through the Bridge Tunnel channel. Once in open water the wind still only five knots meant motoring would be the rule. If you can't sail five knots, might as well motor. Entering the shipping lanes during the night is always a precarious situation; you can see them, but they do not always see you. Even with radar, someone may not be alert. Once again, Murphy's Law came into play. My radar showed a freighter coming at us on an intersecting course. I hailed the bridge on the marine radio, fully expecting a response, nothing.

I did this repeatedly as I watched the monster bearing down on us. Within a quarter of a mile of our position, I made a 180 degree turn around as a defensive maneuver. I knew if I kept the course, the freighter would be eating my hull for lunch. As luck would have it, someone in the wheelhouse must have woken up, because the freighter made a hard turn to port. The ship was roughly 800 hundred feet long and empty; thankfully, she showed her screws and the wash kicked up some chop that sent Mike out of the bunk onto the cabin sole. He did not so much as stir from the jolt. We continued to motor a good part of the evening to our first course change to the South-Southeast. The wind finally came up and we sailed quietly through the rest of the night.

Sunshine blessed us on the third day of our passage when we were three hundred miles off the coast. However, alas, there was no wind, so we took advantage of the moment to swim in approximately 15,000 feet of water. The ocean was like a lake, flat, no waves, no wind. Mike noticed some small fin like fish just floating along. Not knowing what they were, we climbed back into the cockpit for a better view. To our surprise, they were Portuguese Man-o-war jellyfish. The swim was an exhilarating experience, we could see down about ten feet into the ocean and anything after that was a deep blue to black into the depths of darkness.

Now that we were essentially halfway to Bermuda, I had the idea to celebrate. Remember that I had told Mike the sail would be completely dry. I had, however, failed mention that I had stashed bottles of alcoholic beverage throughout the boat, in various and sundry nooks and crannies of storage space, including three cases of beer stashed under the forward bunk. Mike, bless his trusting heart, had no idea how devious I could be.

"Hey, Mike how about we celebrate our making it halfway and have a Virgin Mary with celery?"

"You're killing me!"

"Come on, think of it as a teaser for the island when we can make up for the withdrawals."

"Withdrawal is putting the last three days without a Guinness mildly!"

In the galley, I made some not-so-virgin Marys with an appreciable amount of Vodka. Handing him one, with a toast.

"Cheers, brother, here's to Bermuda!" He proceeded to take a whopping slug of what he thought was tomato juice and his eyes got as big as golf balls.

"You son of a bitch, there is Vodka in this virgin!"

I smiled, lifting the glass in toast, saying "You deserve it brother, for putting up with my dry sail subterfuge."

We reverted to the dry rule for the rest of the trip, and food was not as plentiful as we would have liked. Although Mike loved to fish, his attempt to catch anything we could grill was unsuccessful. He was below when the rod he had placed off the stern started to bend. He came flying out of the cabin fully expecting to see something worth eating on his line.

When a foreign object resembling a telephone pole appeared on the end of the line, we were both disappointed, Mike bearing the look of a kid who dropped his ice cream from a cone.

Chapter 7

"Anyone can hold the helm when the sea is calm."

Publilius Syrus

Going with the Flow

The day after our dip in the ocean, the weather was favorable, so we set sail again. I had been taking GPS coordinates and preparing to chart our position, course, and speed over ground for the boat's log. Mike called out to me. "Hey Frank, you're not going to believe this come out here." I joined him and he pointed to the compass. The damn thing was spinning like a top. We both smiled and then realized our position, on the outer margins of the Bermuda Triangle, the tales of which are numerous and legendary.

We stood transfixed, watching the compass change course heading and spin, then show us a totally different heading.

"No problem I will use the GPS to get a heading." The expression on my face made Mike laugh.

"Don't tell me the GPS isn't working," he said in disbelief.

"OK, I won't tell you."

He told me to turn all the electronics on; nothing was working from radios to radar. "Where's Gilligan when we need him?," I wondered aloud, "This must be our three-hour tour. The Navy will find two skeletons floating around the triangle or we will disappear never to be seen or heard from again."

"It will be fine; it is still daylight, and the sky is clear. Everything will go back to normal in a few minutes an hour at most," Mike reassured me.

"Well, we at least know where we are. Keep the sun on the port quarter and when the moon rises if nothing is working, we can guesstimate from that."

That is exactly what happened. None of the instruments, electronics or the compass came back to life. In a sense we were sailing blindfolded and by feel. Lost in the triangle, I could almost hear Rod Serling narrating the beginning of a *Twilight Zone* episode. "Two friends on the adventure of a lifetime sailing to a small island in the middle of the Atlantic Ocean, unbeknownst to them they are sailing into the unknown, destined to follow a compass that leads them to nowhere..." (cue music)

We checked the electronics sporadically throughout the night; still nothing. It was eerie, yet strangely comforting to have no recourse other than to let it be. The ocean is the ultimate metaphor for life and at that moment, the bumper sticker slogan "just go with the flow" took on a literal meaning.

At dawn, the sun rose off the left or port side of the boat; that meant we had sailed in a general Southerly direction through the night. Given the boat's speed, we likely traveled about one hundred miles deeper into the triangle and off course. In the grand scheme of things, it was not terrible, the ocean is vast. By mid-morning, the boat came back to life we hooped and howled, our arms pumping the sky. "We are back in business," I said, checking our position and giving Mike the course changes.

A day and a half from the island the winds were consistently in the 20 to 30 knot range blowing from the east-northeast. The seas averaging nine feet and tightly packed put Anastasia to the task of taking a repeated pounding as she crested waves and fell into the trough. Mike got a workout, keeping her on an upwind course, as she sailed on her ear.

Mike said, "She has a bone in her teeth now!"

As the knot meter clicked off nine knots, sometimes 10.5 knots, we cascaded down into the face of some waves burying the bow in the trough. *Anastasia* kept beating along, her rigging whistling, and her hull humming from the cavitation of her wake. I was jolted awake regularly by crashing sounds, flashing back to my ill-fated departure the previous year, when caught in a storm front. Jumping out of the rack, I yelled out to Mike. "What just broke?"

"Nothing! This is *sailing*! Go back to sleep," Mike responded.

After the third or fourth time that I jumped up, Mike yelled "go back to sleep" before I could even make a move to rise. I heard him laughing at me from the cockpit.

We spent the night back winded at the Northern waypoint of the island. The usual regimen was our twelve-hour communications with Jessie and Greg back at the marina in Hampton, Virginia. The weather, our position, condition of the boat, and the general goings on were required conversation.

The next morning, we woke up with the island in view. We were full steam ahead until we made an accidental jibe. The travel car broke, the very one I had replaced the previous year.

"Holy crap!" Mike said, grabbing the boom to stop it from swinging away. "Good thing there isn't a strong breeze!"

I just shook my head with raised eyebrows and chuckled along with him. We used a spare genoa car and took the slide car off the track for the headsail, essentially robbing from Peter to pay Paul. After about an hour, we were back in business and on our way.

Chapter 8

"You can go to heaven if you want to. I'd rather stay in Bermuda"

Mark Twain

Paradise Found

Arriving in Bermuda, our first order of business was to check in through the harbormaster's office and customs. Once done, we found a small marina tucked away from the maddening crowd of tourists. First on the agenda was meat, juicy bloody meat, burgers and fries and a tall cold beer. All of which we found at the first restaurant we came across. "Two large medium rare cheeseburgers with fries and the biggest glass of beer you got, please." We both had the widest of grins on our faces, reveling in the fact that we had reached our destination in one piece.

Mike's already adventurous spirit was stimulated by the trip over; mine was satisfied. I had brought Judith's ashes with me to release in the harbor, providing me with much-needed closure.

Our tummies full, Mike and I went back to the boat, weaving down the road, from the quantity of beer combined with our residual sea legs. I went below to unload my extensive stash of liquor and beer. Mike was utterly amazed at how much booze was secretly stowed. We relaxed at a picnic table at the marina looking at the few boats docked alongside us and became acquainted with our island mates. This included a family of four with two children under the age of three and one crewmember. They had been cruising for the past year and were now on their last leg home. Also present were a father and son who bought a boat in the islands and were sailing back home to England with two friends as crew. We also met the crew from an impressive 85-foot sailboat whose homeport was none other than Newport, Rhode Island, my old stomping ground. Then there was Mike and me; two wild and crazy adrenaline aficionados. Although a motley and eclectic crew, we all fit quite nicely together, fellow travelers on the ocean sharing a brief respite in paradise.

That evening with the grill fired up we cooked all the meat and fish a sailor could dream of. Coupled with a beautiful array of tropical fruit, bottles of beer, wine, and liquor from every stash on every boat, it was a scene straight from a Fellini film. By the time the music blared out over the harbor, other boaters had joined the festivities, adding more bottles and food. It was a floating Woodstock, with no law enforcement to be seen or heard.

Mike and I did some touristy stuff for a few days, renting scooters to experience (and photograph) the beauty of the island. We also made a special trip to a boat yard where some vessels had been left behind or damaged from hurricanes. Our mission was to find a traveler car to replace the one that had broken after we accidentally jibed the boat at the northern mark.

Socializing with a young man named Chris and his dad who were on layover heading to the Azores was a wistful encounter. Visiting the Azores was on my bucket list, and Judith and I had hoped to do so before she passed.

"Come with us Frank, follow behind, tag along, it will be a glorious adventure!" they said, nudging me to join them in the jaunt. They spent the better part of an hour giving all the details on the journey and reinforcing the adventure and cajoling me.

"You two don't know what you are tickling me with."

"Yes, we do!" they laughed, "Just come!"

"I will get there someday, just not now."

"No, you never will," Chris warned. "You will go back to the States and fall into the routine of working and forget about the dreams for an adventurous life."

Chris's dad agreed with his comment by nodding his head and in his best British accent vocalized, "He's right you know!"

"In my heart I have the sense you may both be right. Time will tell."

With this short visit nearing to a close, I mentally prepared for my return trip to the states in a few days. On Sunday, Mike flew back to Virginia. Now the final preparations for my departure entailed refueling and repairing the wind-steering unit.

I bid my new friends a fond adieu and girded my loins for the trip back.

Chapter 9

"On a day when the wind is perfect, the sail just needs to open, and the world is full of beauty."

Rumi

The Way Back

On the morning of my sail back, I followed the same protocol as when we arrived. After going to the harbor master's office and getting my port papers, I radioed Harbor Tower to get permission to leave. I sat patiently in the water, motor on, waiting for the green light.

The first part of the journey back was pleasant and uneventful in terms of turbulence. I sailed among large ships, one of which looked like a Spanish Galleon. Things were calm, and I was able to cook and relax, enjoying the scenery.

Later, warning of an approaching storm reached me via single side band radio. To prepare, I deployed my gale rider off the bow using my anchor chain and rode and set the storm sail. I kept an eye on the storm system bearing down on my position at the predicted thirty to thirty-five mile per hour pace. I had traveled for a couple of hours under motor after hearing the report in hopes of putting myself well off its eastern side. That method served me well; the lead front went by me with winds in the low twenties and the seas around five to seven feet in a regular pattern. I was ready for the big roller-coaster ride from expected thirty to forty-knot winds and seas predicted fifteen feet or more. As I sat in the cockpit watching the low dark clouds move on by, I got antsy.

"I should be sailing, not sitting here," I said aloud, "I have sailed in worse."

I then performed the exhausting and arduous task of retrieving the 250 feet of line and chain attached to the gale rider. The entire process would have been smoother had I put a trip line on the ring to make it easier to haul in. Leaving the storm sail in place, I raised the main with one reef and sailed along the Eastern side of the front as it passed off to the southwest.

The actual storm presented itself later that evening. The front was so low in the sky I could have reached up and touched the blackened clouds stretching to the horizon in either direction before me. The winds had already begun to push the thirty-knot level, leaving me no choice but to stay put in the cockpit with two thirds of my sail plan flying. I pointed *Anastasia* into the wind as tight as I could and still make way lying down in the cockpit under the dodger to keep dry from the pounding rain. While the gusts ran the gamut up and down the thirty-forty-five knot range, I prayed and *Anastasia* took a pounding, shuddering, and creaking from the strain of the wind and waves.

Not taking any chances, the ditch bag was in place on the rail, the EPIRB was ready and at hand, along with my handheld VHF. The life raft was pulled from the lazaret and tied to the rear rail in the cockpit. Sailing in that type of weather is, in a word, unpredictable, so I was prepared for every possible calamity.

As I lay quietly in the cockpit listening to the torrent around me, something hit me in the back. I thought it was a flying fish, but it turned out to be a small greyish brown bird with a black ring on its neck cooing like a dove as it fluttered its wings on my back. "Oh great, another monkey in the wrench," I thought. I was able to coddle it with my two hands and send it on its way, so I hoped. However, it appeared again the next morning, this time on a blanket in my cockpit. There I was, 200+ miles off the coast with a little bird from nowhere joining me for the ride. I fed it some bread and we continued a conversation for the next 24 hours, while it stayed huddled in the folds of the blanket. Approaching the Gulf Stream, my compass spun out of control, my wind indicator following suit within minutes, then the GPS joined in. I asked the bird if we should just follow the setting sun and hope for the best. Cooing, the bird seemed to think it was a good plan, so I did just that. Then without notice the bird flew off into the horizon, with me watching and saying, "Safe home!" At that point, motion atop the water caught my eye and I saw a couple of Dolphins playing in the surf of the boat. "Oh great," I said, "Now Flipper and his buddy are here!" Initially, I thought there were only two of them, but a pod of at least ten or fifteen, surrounded the boat on both sides jumping and playing in the bow wake. During all this time going on nine hours the compass and GPS along with the wind indicator were still non-functional. So, I let the Dolphins direct me; I sailed between them and let them lead the boat. Within the hour, the electronics all came to life again. The Dolphins stayed for another hour before disappearing below the surface.

After another day of sailing, I approached the Chesapeake Bay Bridge tunnel, and motored in heading towards the marina. I called Mike and Jesse and Greg to let them know I was on my way back. By then it was dark, and just as I was about to turn into the alleyway of the marina, I came to a dead halt; the engine quit. The current was starting to go out and the boat was starting to go backwards.

I phoned Mike – "You're not going to believe this."

"What now?"

"I'm out of fuel."

"I *knew* you should have brought extra fuel," he said, clearly reveling in his "I told you so" moment, said "I'll be right there," and promptly came out on his sailboat to tow me in.

As we docked *Anastasia*, friends greeted me warmly, and I was overwhelmed by a feeling of peace and accomplishment.

Sometime after, when Mike and I drank together, sharing memories of the trip, he trotted out his favorite toast, an Irish proverb: ***"There are good ships and wood ships, ships that sail the sea, but the best ships are friendships, may they always be!"***

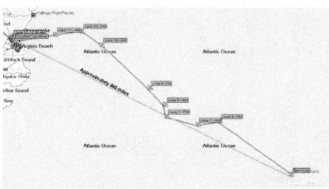

Anastasia Map, Return Trip / see page 64 for enlarged version of map

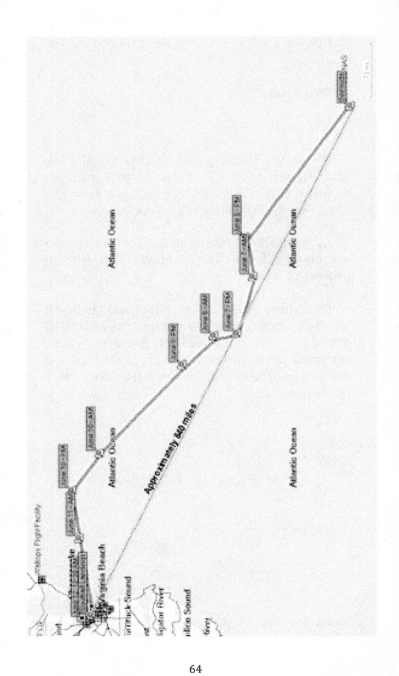

Post-Script

"Adventure isn't hanging on a rope off the side of a mountain. Adventure is an attitude that we must apply to the day-to-day obstacles of life – facing new challenges, seizing new opportunities, testing our resources against the unknown and in the process, discovering our own unique potential."

John Amatt

The joy derived from writing this story was not present in the beginning. Although it had been intended as a beacon of hope for those beset with grief, specifically husbands going through a similar experience, the earlier edition of this book was dark.

It included journal entries laying out every emotion I was feeling; I was a rudderless ship. On its pages I spilled out my anger, despair, sadness, insecurity, as well as intimate details of my marriage. Upon reflection, I realized that the best way to honor my wife's memory was to live my life, despite the uncertainty of what lay ahead. Judith will always be with me in spirit, but I have come to understand that to be fully present, one must be fully engaged. While I have many happy memories, it serves no purpose to idealize the past, if it keeps me in limbo, stuck between two worlds, playing reels of our marriage together on an endless loop. The sail to Bermuda, and authoring this book, have helped me move forward with courage, embrace life, wherever it takes me, making new memories along the way. As the late Gilda Radner said "Life is about not knowing...delicious ambiguity"

My trip to Bermuda was an adventure which shaped the trajectory of my life, and taught me much, some of which I didn't realize until dusting off this manuscript. As the Stones sang, "Time is on my side." In retrospect, as tragic as it was, Judith's death gave me something tangible on which to hang my cloak of depression. It was a dragon to which I could put a name and face, unlike the others that visited me in night terrors, bouts of self-loathing, and even during times that I tried to be happy go lucky. I could relax and embrace life for only so long; like the character Pig-Pen from the *Peanuts* comic strip, the dark cloud was always above me.

The most important lesson that I am still learning from my journey is that it is just as important to receive as it is to give. I was a Knight in Shining

Armor for my late wife but would not afford myself the same vassal. I went down the dark rabbit hole of survivor's guilt. If you believe in the laws of attraction, then you'll understand when I say that I attracted the delays, from the storms to the broken equipment and everything in between, because if the sail was smooth, then I would be getting something I did not deserve. Why should I have a wonderful time, living out a dream that I shared with my wife, when she could not be there with me - *mea culpa, mea culpa, mea maxima culpa.*

A favorite quote from Alice in Wonderland is ""It takes all the running you can do, to keep in the same place. If you want to get somewhere else, you must run at least twice as fast as that!"

However, even when I did not consciously ask for help – it came to me in various forms. The most obvious nudge came from the prodding, enthusiastic and stubborn Mike, who punched me into reality. But boosts of courage and love came from many others who aided and supported me, in ways big and small. In a person's life, it isn't the stack of accomplishments that bring satisfaction of a job well done, it is the effort of giving that holds value above accolade. Intellectually, I knew that the key to living a good life was selflessness without ego, the fibers woven into the fabric of respect and unexpected recognition. Performing random and unconditional acts of kindness for family, friends, and strangers openly and with love is what gives life purpose. Emotionally, I was not quite there yet; what I didn't quite understand was that I owed myself the same unconditional kindness.

Although I did not acknowledge his presence when I wrote this prayer my inner Knight in Shining armor helped me:

> *"Lord Jesus, Son of God, hear my prayer! Bless my soul so I don't lose sight of my spirit in the darkness of the abyss; hold me close, with your breath of spirit, guide me from my weakened heart and brighten me. Amen."*

In these pages, I spoke of the bird who kept me company on my sail back from Bermuda. Initially, I thought it was a flying fish. Then I assumed it was a visitation from Judith. In retrospect, I know that it was a visitation from a higher power telling me that we are never alone; as John Donne wrote "no man is an island entire of itself; every man is a piece of the continent, a part of the main." So, maybe a "solo sail" was never possible because we are all on earth to guide and help each other. When recounting the bird story during the reworking of this book, I mentioned that it was just a "poor little creature lost in a storm who didn't know where else to go." I'm a little dense at times; I was talking about myself.

In another chapter, I wrote about fellow travelers who invited me to visit the Azores with them. When I declined, saying "I will get there someday," they refuted that statement. "It's now or never," they admonished. At that time, I concurred, saying "In my heart I have the sense...you may be right. Time will tell."

As of this writing, seventeen years after that conversation, I have still never been to the Azores.

However, my fascination with the region led me to write a soon to be published novel, *The Pearls*. Giacomo, the protagonist, is a sailor from the Azores. Roman a clef? Indubitably! Giacomo loves sailing, craves danger, loses his wife, survives many perils, and will be featured in a sequel. Coincidentally, my life story also has a sequel in progress. I am slowly clearing paths, both literally and metaphorically, to build a new home and studio. Details to be provided on a need-to-know basis.

As for *Anastasia,* we parted ways when my life took a different turn. Once again, it was a bittersweet goodbye. Had it not been for *Anastasia*, I would not have fulfilled a promise, but it was time to move on and to stop living between two worlds. Things didn't always go perfectly during the post-*Anastasia* period; some new dreams were dashed, some new challenges presented. Surviving the good the bad and the ugly is a reminder that I have a lot more living to do, and that every day is a new beginning. Some might call it luck, some a blessing; I'm not sure myself. But I suspect that it is largely because I refuse to live in boxes, never willing to square off the edges of my kingdom of imaginings. My editor believes that the most important lesson one needs to learn in life is that "anything is possible." She is almost correct; the truth is that everything is possible. New adventures await!

God bless.

About Frank J. DiMaio, Author

Photo Credit Tallulah Gillbride

Born and raised in Rhode Island, Frank J. DiMaio has lived a storied and eclectic life, full of twists and turns. He grew up in the restaurant business, working at his parents' diner where the featured menu item was N.Y. system wieners, a Rhode Island staple. This engendered both a strong work ethic and a love of food, which is why all of Frank's works have eating scenes. His recipe for deer shoulder earned him a spot on a local cooking show when he lived in Virginia. Now leaning towards vegetarianism, he is obsessed with kale, although he occasionally enjoys a slab of beef at his favorite watering hole near his home in Florida.

Although Frank's self-deprecating nature makes him uncomfortable with the label "Renaissance Man," there is no other way to describe him. After enjoying a successful practice as a Chiropractic Physician for more than a decade, a freak accident forced him to give up his practice, so his career path changed direction. He then studied landscape architectture which eventually led him to sculpting. His work is in private collections in the U.S. and Canada. He also draws and paints, is an award-winning photographer, and a former member of a Barbershop Chorus, and learned to play saxophone when he lived across the hall from students attending the Boston Conservatory of Music. To support his art, he has worked on tugboats, as an aide with autistic children, at an airport, and as a line cook and assistant kitchen manager for a large steak house chain. A restless soul with "sand in his shoes," Frank has lived in and traveled through several states including Colorado, New Mexico, and Virginia, and lived in Canada for ten years. He now resides in Florida, where he is designing and building a home and studio.

The Best Ships is his first book with others in queue, including *The Pearls*, an adventure story set during the Opium Wars, *Letters from the Trenches*,

The Continuing Adventures of Comma Boy, and *Tales from the Couch*. He is also developing a blog on the psychology of healing.

Frank holds a Bachelor of Arts degree in Psychology from Providence College, his Doctorate from New York Chiropractic College, and a Master of Science degree from Troy State University. Frank also sometimes uses the pseudonym Francesco James for his sculpture, photography and certain writing projects.

About Vicki Lindgren Rimasse, Collaborator and Editor

Photo Credit Francesco James

Vicki Lindgren Rimasse has been writing for most of her life. After law school, she worked as a legal writer and editor, and over the years has often ghostwritten and edited works for many authors, most of whom shall remain nameless. The popularity of her blog, *The Divamom Love Food and Shopping Blog* led her to publish *Ruminations of a Catholic School Girl (Who Thinks in Latin, but Lives Near Hackensack)*, a best-selling compendium of humor essays. In addition to working on her second book, *Too Many Mooks, Too Little Time*, she is currently collaborating with author Frank Dimaio on various works, including Letters *from the Trenches*, an adventure-romance set during World War I. Originally from Long Island, Vicki is currently exiled to Suburban Purgatory in the Northern New Jersey suburbs, from which she is planning her escape. Her fantasy is to live in Tuscany, where she can drink wine and philosophize with other writers and artists but would settle for any state where she will not be immediately outed as a former New Yorker based on her penchant for wearing black and her fluency in sarcasm.

Vicki earned a Bachelor of Science in Behavioral Sciences from NY Institute of Technology, and her J.D. from Hofstra University School of Law. She is a member of Toastmasters International and has competed in (and occasionally won) various club and area level contests.

Glossary

Boom: A spar (pole), along the foot of a fore and aft rigged sail, that greatly improves control of the angle and shape of the sail.

Bow: the front part of the hull.

Catamaran: a vessel, usually propelled by sail, formed of two hulls or floats held side by side by a frame above them

Companionway: a stairway or ladder leading from one deck to another in a boat or ship

Deck: The deck is a part of the boat that sits on top of the hull.

Dinghy: A lifeboat found on board of a ship in case of emergency

Halyard: a halyard or halliard is a line (rope) that is used to hoist a ladder, sail, flag, or yard.

Jib: The sail at the front of the boat. It increases a sailboat's speed by adding sail area which catches more wind.

A Jibe (US) or Gybe (Britain) is a sailing maneuver whereby a sailing vessel reaching downwind turns its stern through the wind, which then exerts its force from the opposite side of the vessel

Genoa sail or genoa car: A type of large jib or staysail that extends past the mast and so overlaps the main sail when viewed from the side, sometimes eliminating it.

Hatch: An opening that connects the bottom of the boat and the deck.

Helm: A wheel that is used to control the direction of the boat.

Hull: The actual body or shell of a boat that includes several different parts of the structure, such as the deck, the bottom, and the sides.

Keel: The keel is a specific part of the hull. It is the main beam that runs from the front (bow) of the boat to the back (stern) and goes through the middle of the vessel.

Leach: Leech – The aft (back) edge of a fore-and-aft sail is called the leach (also spelled leach). It is on either side edge of a symmetrical sail—triangular or square.

Line: A line is another word for rope in the nautical realm.

Mainsheet Traveler: Also called a "travel car," the mainsheet traveler is a device that allows for changing the position where the mainsheet tackle connects to the boat.

Mast: is a tall spar, or arrangement of spars, erected vertically on the centerline of a ship or boat.

Pontoon: a small a metal structure used specially to form or support a temporary floating bridge

Port: The left side of a boat, when you're facing forward or toward the bow, is known as port.

Rigging: The lines (ropes) that are used to work the masts, yards, and sails. When a person is going up into the rigging, it is often referred to as "going aloft."

Rudder: part of the steering apparatus of a boat or ship that is fastened outside the hull, usually at the stern.

Spreader: A spar on a sailboat used to deflect the shrouds to allow them to better support the mast.

Starboard: The right side of a boat, when you're facing forward or toward the bow, is known as starboard.

Stern: The back part of the vessel. When a person is moving toward the stern, they are moving aft. However, if the boat is moving backward, it is called astern. When facing the bow of the ship but standing in the stern, the left side is called the port quarter while the right side is considered the starboard quarter.

Tiller: a lever used to turn the rudder of a boat from side to side broadly.

Vang: A boom vang (US) is a line or piston system on a sailboat used to exert downward force on the boom and thus control the shape of the sail.

CPSIA information can be obtained
at www.ICGtesting.com
Printed in the USA
BVHW080636061121
620961BV00005B/175